HEALING:
INSIDE OUT AND OUTSIDE IN

FINDING PEACE THROUGH SPIRITUAL HEALING

Gwendolyn Miller,
MA, LPC-MHSP

Terms and Conditions

LEGAL NOTICE

Prioritizing self-care is essential in today's fast-paced world. This book serves as a resource to encourage reflection, well-being, and informed decision-making. While every effort has been made to provide accurate and useful information, the rapidly changing nature of the Internet means that some content may evolve over time.

The Publisher does not assume responsibility for errors, omissions, or varying interpretations of the material. Any unintended misrepresentations or perceived slights against individuals, groups, or organizations are purely coincidental.

While self-care strategies can be beneficial, they are not a substitute for professional guidance. If you are facing challenges that require expert advice—whether in mental health, legal matters, business, accounting, or finance—seeking help from qualified professionals is always recommended.

Your well-being matters. Take the time to care for yourself, and don't hesitate to reach out for support when needed.

For convenience, you are welcome to print this book for easier reading.

CONTENTS

Foreword 5

Chapter 1: Mindfulness Exercises 7

Chapter 2: Words of Spiritual Encouragement ... 13

Chapter 3: Day-to-Day Affirmation 19

Chapter 4: Communities 24

Chapter 5: Spiritual Cleansing 28

Chapter 6: Spiritual Thinkings 39

Chapter 7: Forgiving Other People 47

Chapter 8: Attitude of Appreciation 60

Wrapping Up 65

About the Author 67

FOREWORD

Practicing spiritual wellness is the key to living a life of fulfillment, success, peace, love, prosperity, and joy.

All the same, you don't get to this level of enlightenment overnight. It calls for discipline, but the advantages are definitely worth the effort you put into it.

So what are a few of these practices? There are a lot of them but these are some of the most crucial ones.

CHAPTER 1

Mindfulness Exercises

Synopsis

It's crucial to listen to the silence on a regular basis. Being still allows you to be present in the moments. When practicing mindfulness, as a Christian, I use the scriptures as my foundational approach. For example, *Psalms 46:10 says, He says, "Be still, and know that I am God; I will be exalted among the nations, I will be exalted in the earth."* The outside world is filled with too much discombobulation. You have to learn to pay attention to the Divine Voice inside and learn to trust His Voice. It's likewise useful to practice being in the here and now. The practice of mindfulness may bring a lot of advantages to your emotional and physical health, as well as to the relationships in your life. Mindfulness is about being aware and observing what is happening in one's thoughts, senses, emotions, and surroundings. Additionally, mindfulness is learning how to accept what is happening in the present moment without judgment. When teaching this aspect of mindfulness, I share Matthew 22: 37-40, Jesus replied: "'Love the Lord your God with all your heart and with all your soul and with all your mind.' This is the first and greatest commandment. And the second is like it: 'Love your neighbor as yourself.'

All the Law and the Prophets hang on these two commandments." In all, mindfulness is connected to learning how to accept you are loved by the one who created you, loving yourself because you were created out of love and for love, and lastly, loving others as yourself.

Mindfulness is an astounding tool for stress management and overall wellness as it may be used at virtually any time and may quickly bring lasting results. The following mindfulness exercises are easy and convenient, and may lead you to a deeper experience of mindfulness in your daily life.

Be Mindful

Meditation

Meditation brings a lot of advantages in its own right and has been one of the most popular and traditional ways to accomplish mindfulness for centuries, so it tops the list of mindfulness exercises. Meditation gets to be easier with practice, but it need not be hard for beginners. Simply discover a comfortable place, free of distractions, and calm your mind.

Deep Breathing

That's correct: mindfulness may be as easy as breathing! Seriously, though, among the most uncomplicated ways to experience mindfulness, which may be done as you go about your day-to-day activities (convenient for those who feel they don't have time to meditate), is to center on your breathing.

Gwendolyn Miller, MA, LPC-MHSP

Breathe from your belly instead of from your chest, and try to inhale through your nose, hold your breath for a few seconds, and then exhale out through your mouth. Centering on the sound and rhythm of your breath, particularly when you are upset, may have a calming effect and help you stay grounded in the here and now.

Listening to Music

Listening to music has a lot of advantages — so many, as a matter of fact, that music is being utilized therapeutically in a fresh branch of complementary medicine known as music therapy. That's part of why listening to music makes an excellent mindfulness exercise.

You are able to play soothing jazz music, classical music, gospel music, or a different type of slow-tempo music to feel calming effects, and make it an exercise in mindfulness by truly centering on the sound and vibration of every note, the feelings that the music brings up inside you, and additional sensations that are happening "right now" as you listen. If additional thoughts creep into your brain, congratulate yourself for noticing, and gently bring your attention back to the present moment and the music you're hearing.

Housecleaning

The term "housecleaning" has a literal meaning (cleaning up your actual house) as well as a non-literal one (doing away with "emotional baggage", letting go of things that non longer serve you), and both may be great stress relievers! Because clutter has several hidden costs and may be a subtle but significant stressor, housecleaning and decluttering as a mindfulness exercise may bring lasting benefits.

To bring mindfulness to cleaning, you first have to view it as a positive event, a drill in self-understanding and stress relief, instead of merely as a chore. Then, as you clean, center on what you're doing as you're doing it — and nothing else.

Feel the warm, soapy water on your hands as you rinse dishes; experience the vibrations of the vacuum as you cover the area of the floor; enjoy the warmth of the laundry as you fold it; feel the freedom of relinquishing unneeded objects as you put them in the donations bag. It might sound a bit silly as you read it here, but if you approach cleaning as a drill in mindfulness, it may become one.

Honoring Your Thoughts

A lot of stressed and busy individuals find it hard to stop centering on the rapid stream of thoughts consuming their mind, and the idea of sitting in meditation and holding off the onslaught of thought may really cause more stress! If this sounds like you, the mindfulness drill of observing your thoughts may be for you. Instead of working against the voice in your head, you sit back and "honor" your thoughts, instead of becoming involved in them. As you notice them, you may find your mind calming, and the thoughts becoming less stressful. If you struggle with constantly thinking, you are not alone. You are in good company with me and many others. So, I have learned when thoughts are "interfering" with my desire to be silent, I acknowledge the thought and bring it back to whatever I was originally focusing on.

Make Your Own!

You're likely now getting the idea that virtually any activity may be a mindfulness exercise, and in a way, you're correct. It helps to practice meditation or a different exercise that truly centers on mindfulness, but you are able to bring mindfulness to anything you do, and find yourself less stressed and more grounded in the procedure. In all, the goal is to learn how to merge mindfulness into your everyday life.

CHAPTER 2

Words of Spiritual Encouragement

Synopsis

Studying the Bible and listening to messages from Bible-based ministers can help you stay focused and strengthen your faith. These resources are valuable companions that you can carry with you wherever you go and incorporate into your daily life.

When I talk about spiritual growth, I mean learning to apply biblical teachings to your everyday experiences—a journey that can sometimes be challenging. In those moments, words of spiritual encouragement can provide the comfort and guidance you need to keep moving forward.

The Gift Of Words

Wherever you're on your journey, scripture verses and uplifting quotes may make it easier for you to continue on your path. I've been on a disciple of Jesus for over 20 years. I can't count the number of times that I've turned to Bible verses to help me restore my faith. They're powerful tools that I turn to over and over again. Remember, Ephesians 6:17 says that the word of God is the sword of the Spirit, so using the word helps us to battle against intrusive, negative thoughts.

I'm honored to share some of the wisdom quotes from some of my *battle scriptures* that have helped me over the years. Read these inspirational expressions, savor them, and let them fill your heart with hope.

Spiritual Encouragement Self-Esteem

"I praise you because I am fearfully and wonderfully made; your works are wonderful." (Psalms 139:14) *(Breath in "I am fearfully and wonderfully made". Exhale "I am wonderful.")*

"Since you are precious and honored in my sight, and because I love you." (Isaiah 43:4) *(Breath in "I am precious and honored in God's sight". Exhale "God loves me.")*

Spiritual Encouragement About Confidence

"I can do all this through him who gives me strength." Phil 4:13 *(Breath in "I can do all this"- Exhale "through him who gives me strength.)*

"For the Spirit God gave us does not make us timid, but gives us power, love and self-discipline." 2 Timothy 1:7 *(Breath in "For God has not given me a spirit of fear"- Exhale "but of power, love, and self-discipline")*

"But blessed is the one who trusts in the Lord, whose confidence is in him." (Jeremiah 17:7) *(Breath in "I trust in you Lord."- Exhale "my confidence is in you.")*

"Have I not commanded you? Be strong and courageous. Do not be afraid; do not be discouraged, for the Lord your God will be with you wherever you go." (Joshua 1:9) *(Breath in "Be strong and courageous"- Exhale "God is with me.")*

Spiritual Encouragement About Faith

"But those who hope in the Lord will renew their strength: They will soar on wings like eagles; they will run and not grow weary, they will walk and not be faint." (Isaiah 40:31) *(Breath in "I trust you Lord - Exhale "The Lord renews my strength."*

"And we know that in all things God works for the good of those who love him, who have been called according to his purpose." (Romans 8:28) *(Breath in "God is always at work - Exhale "Working for my good.")*

"I will lead the blind by ways they have not known, along unfamiliar paths I will guide them; I will turn the darkness into light before them and make the rough places smooth. These are the things I will do; I will not forsake them. (Isaiah 42:16) *(Breath in "Though I can't see my way" - Exhale "The Lord is guiding me and won't leave me alone."*

Spiritual Encouragement About Love

"The Lord appeared to us in the past, saying: 'I have loved you with an everlasting love; I have drawn you with loving-kindness." (Jeremiah 31:3) *(Breath in "God loves me" - Exhale "With an everlasting love.")*

"And so we know and rely on the love God has for us. God is love. Whoever lives in love lives in God, and God in him." (1 John 4:16) *(Breath in "God is love" - Exhale "I will live in love and live in God.")*

"We love because he first loved us." (1 John 4:19) *(Breath in "I love myself and others - Exhale "Because God loved me first.")*

"But God demonstrated his own love for us in this: While we were still sinners, Christ died for us." (Romans 5:8) *(Breath in "God demonstrated his love for me, a sinner" - Exhale "By sending his Son to die for me.")*

I sincerely hope the scriptures and the breathing meditations have been helpful for you. I invite you to read them frequently.

CHAPTER 3

Day-to-Day Affirmation

Synopsis

Saying a day-to-day affirmation is an excellent way to stay in a state of spiritual wellness. You and I are so bombed with negativity day after day. Positive and healing affirmations may help you feel better about your life and more optimistic about your future.

Use Affirmations

A lot of individuals ask me if saying a daily affirmation on a consistent basis may make a positive difference in their lives. The answer is decidedly YES.

Gwendolyn Miller, MA, LPC-MHSP

What is a day-to-day affirmation? It's a positive idea of something you would like to believe about yourself which you don't believe today. For example, if you would like to trust that you're confident about your ability to handle yourself in any state of affairs but you don't believe that today, a great daily affirmation maybe – —I'm now confident that I may successfully handle all states of affairs in my life.

Healing: Inside Out And Outside In

We all talk to ourselves each day. A lot of the things we tell ourselves are damaging and limiting. They prevent us from executing things and having things that we truly want in our lives.

A positive affirmation begins to get you to alter your ideas about yourself and what is possible in your life. It's essentially a form of positive self-talk that you're utilizing on a steady basis. You're training your mind to think differently about yourself. Affirmation rules of thumb. It is positive - An affirmation has to be positive. If you're shy, you would not say that you are no longer shy. You wish to affirm what you do wish, not what you don't wish. Utilizing healing affirmations like, ―I am really comfortable when I am with individuals,‖ or ―I may easily talk to new individuals‖, are good example* of affirmations that you may utilize.

It is utilized in the present tense – Words of affirmation have to be said in the present tense. You're affirming in the present tense what you would like to believe about yourself in the future. Your subconscious mind takes what you state about yourself literally. If you continually tell yourself ―I'm smart and I learn new things easily‖, eventually you'll discover that you're able to comprehend fresh ideas easily and without conflict.

It ought to be done on a steady basis – You are attempting to change your unconscious thoughts about yourself with favorable self-talk. This isn't going to occur overnight. You have to say your positive affirmation on a steady basis for it to have any affect. It is really an excellent idea to pick out a daily affirmation and say it to yourself a lot of times throughout the day so it starts to seep down into your subconscious thinking. Ways to discover ideas for words of affirmation – you are able to utilize words of spiritual encouragement or inspirational sayings to help you develop a day-to-day affirmation.

For example, the inspirational idea that there is no limit to what the mind may conceive and accomplish may be turned into —I am able to easily and successfully accomplish anything I set my mind to. Additionally, you can use the scripture from *Philippians 4:13 which says, "I can do all things through Christ who strengthens me."*

Assortment is fine, but take it slowly – you are able to utilize a different one for assorted aspects of your life. You are able to say one for health, one for your job, one for your relationships, one for your finances, or any additional things that are significant to you. Just be aware to take it slowly and not overpower yourself. Your thoughts about yourself are the result of a lot of years of thinking a particular way. It is going to take some time to alter your thinking.

Pick out a few that you wish to work with and stick to them till you feel they are working for you. Then you are able to let those go and work with others. I have used index cards to help me with this process. On one side of the card, I wrote the thoughts and on the other side I wrote the scripture. You can also write the affirmation you want to use that's connected with the scripture. Then, put it on your mirror and say it out loud each day. Remember, It's an Ongoing Process!

Stating a daily affirmation isn't something that you do for a week, a month, or a couple of months -- at least not if you're serious about altering your life for the better. It's a tool that you ought to continue to use on a regular basis. Your life is an expression of your thoughts. Utilize healing affirmations to alter your negative thoughts so you are able to make your life a whole lot better.

CHAPTER 4

Communities

Synopsis

Being with other who are striving to use the Bible in their day to day life is among the best things you are able to do to maintain an attitude of spiritual wellness. A lot of individuals are so centered on the material aspects of life. They believe connecting with Jesus is something you only do one day a week and prayer or reading the Bible is something you do in emergencies.

Seek out like-minded individuals so you are able to learn and grow in your walk with Jesus..

The Right People

Today while I was working and chatting with some acquaintances, I brought up some ideas. Turns out that one acquaintance had the same idea and had in reality, started acting on it. We began talking about it and now a fresh project is now in the works. It made me think just how crucial it is that you have to have the correct individuals beside you. Now don't go thinking that you ought to surround yourself with just —Yes Men as you'll certainly fail when somebody tells you it's a great idea to do something really stupid!

Gwendolyn Miller, MA, LPC-MHSP

Having individuals who think differently and individuals who think alike are equally as crucial to getting a decision made. If the individuals are in a team with you, you need to make certain they're there for your success as well as their own. I have a few individuals in my life who take a valued interest in my success. And there are on both sides of the coin as far as the thought procedure goes. There's obviously my family, my church family, my friends, and colleagues who want me to do well.

And then a few close acquaintances of mine believe very differently from me, but still wish me to genuinely succeed. I value my relationships and expect my friends to tell me when I am off base. Proverbs 27:17 says, "As iron sharpens iron, so one man sharpens another." Also, Proverbs 13:20 says, "He who walks with the wise grows wise, but a companion of fools suffers harm." I am completely aware of who I allow in my life because the people you surround yourself with is who you will eventually become. 1 Corinthians 15:33 says, "Do not be misled: 'Bad company corrupts good character.'"

My acquaintances I hang out with have a similar thought processes like mine. We like the same things. When we are struggling with something, we listen to each other and share scriptures and words of encouragement with one another. We support each other's walk with Jesus and dreams we have for our lives.

Healing: Inside Out And Outside In

To sum it all up you have to have like-minded individuals on both sides of you. The like-minded part comes in mind when we talk about moving you forward in accomplishing your goal and spiritual wellness. If you align yourself with people, make certain that there is a goal to help you draw closer to Jesus and not away from Him and that they want to see you be successful in every part of your life. One last key is that the individuals around you ought to always motivate you to do what is right and move ahead! What types of individuals do you want in your team and how does it impact what you do?

CHAPTER 5

Spiritual Cleansing

Synopsis

It's crucial to pay attention to your thoughts and to let go of those that are damaging and limiting. You need to replace them with ideas of Truth – ideas about God's love and blessings that are available for you. It's crucial for you to release ideas that don't serve you.

Biblically Cleaning

Spiritual cleansing is a process of seeking God's renewal and removing anything that hinders our relationship with Him. The Bible teaches that sin, worldly influences, and spiritual battles can weigh us down, but through prayer, repentance, and God's Word, we can walk in purity and in freedom.

True spiritual cleansing in Christ

Psalm 51:10 – *"Create in me a clean heart, O God, and renew a right spirit within me."*

In life, we encounter struggles that can weigh us down—sin, negativity, and spiritual battles that leave us feeling burdened. The world offers many solutions for cleansing the soul, from meditation to energy readings, but true cleansing comes only from God.

The Bible teaches that when we draw near to God, He draws near to us (James 4:8). Instead of seeking external sources for renewal, we must seek Christ, the **only One who can cleanse, restore, and make us new**. In my life, I have had times when I could tell my heart was not connected to God because of my worldly desires. I was looking at the world and comparing myself with others or desiring to have a relationship with a man who was not pure nor pleasing to God. Even though I have been baptized for the forgiveness of my sins and cleansed and made blemish before Him, my worldly thoughts and desires can draw me away from Jesus and create a distance that I honestly can not stand. Satan tried to use these times to lead me to feel shame and guilt or to think I was unable to change. Can you relate? It is during these times that I have to remember Peter and Judas. Mathew 26:69-75 describes Peter's betrayal of Jesus.

Yes, when we are in sin, we are betraying Jesus.

Healing: Inside Out And Outside In

When we want to do what we want to do and not walk in obedience to Jesus' words, we are betraying him. Peter had walked with Jesus for the 3 years of Jesus' ministry and had the chance to have intimate times with Jesus. Jesus chose him to be one of his closest friends. He even took him with him when he met with Moses and Elijah. Peter had seen it all and yet he still betrayed Jesus. That leads me to question, who are we to think that we can "always" please the Lord. We will mess up and do things that hurt Him, but how are we going to respond? Peter responded by denying Jesus 3 times. Our emotions can lead us in doing things we will regret. Peter was afraid that they would find out he was a disciple of Jesus. He was already witnessing what Jesus was going through as He was being flogged and then crucified. Peter was terrified and allowed his fear to do the one thing he would regret for the rest of his life: Deny the Son of God.

You know the funny thing is that Jesus told Peter he was going to deny him 3 times and that a rooster was going to crow when he does. Peter told Jesus he would never deny him. How many times have I said that I would never do something, but in my heart or in my actions, I did not keep my word. Can you relate?

So, Peter goes on and betrays Jesus, but what does he do after he hears the rooster crow? The scripture says that he ran away weeping bitterly. I can imagine, during this time and after Jesus' death, that Peter went back to fishing because that is where Jesus found him when he came to confront Peter.

In John 21:3-10, it describes their interaction with Jesus when they were fishing, going back to their regular lives after spending time fishing for men with Jesus. Can you imagine the despair, the grief, the regret they must have felt? Peter must have felt? Remember, Peter was the leader of the disciples, so what he did, they did. So Peter led them back to fishing after he had betrayed Jesus. I have to make this point right now. We have to be careful of how we lead especially when we feel guilt, shame, regret, or despair.

As the leader, Peter led the rest of his team away from the mission because he took his eyes off of what he was chosen to do and placed them on himself, his guilt, his regret. What would have happened if Jesus didn't confront them on this day? I wonder.....

Jesus calls Peter to him and asks Peter if he loves him. Jesus asks Peter this 3 times to the point Peter's feelings were hurt on the 3rd time. Each time Jesus asked Peter this, it was reconfirming the commitment Peter had for the mission Jesus called him too and it was reminding Peter of the mission, to feed His sheep and to take care of His lambs. Peter was reinstated back to Jesus on this day because, even though he may have felt guilt, shame, regret, grief, and despair, he did not give up. Also, I think he recognized how much Jesus loved Him and that love led him to accept the forgiveness Jesus was giving him and to let go and forgive himself for the betrayal. He was able to go on and lead the first Church and still continues to impact souls today.

Judas, on the other hand, had the same opportunities as Peter. He also walked with Jesus for 3 years and witnessed everything Jesus was doing in his ministry.

He saw Jesus heal the sick and raise the dead. He was one of the 12 disciples Jesus sent off and they were able to do miracles too! Can you imagine this? Judas had the chance to have a close relationship with Jesus, but his thoughts hindered him. His sin stopped him from being close to Jesus. In the scripture it says that he was stealing money from the resources the disciples had (John 12:6). Ya'll, Jesus even washed Judas' feet knowing he was the one who was going to betray him (John 13:5, 26-27).

Judas, similar to Peter's betrayal, focused on his desires above his relationship with Jesus.

Because of Judas' greed, he betrayed Jesus, but after witnessing all that Jesus went through for him, he regretted his decision. He wanted to take it all back because he knew he had betrayed innocent blood. But, the deed was done. There was nothing more he could do. He felt amazingly guilty and regretful for his decision. He didn't know what to do with this guilt. He didn't remember the love Jesus showed him. He didn't remember the times he spent sitting at the table listening to the Master speak. He was only caught up on his mistakes, his regrets. His thoughts were overwhelmed by this to the point where he didn't see any hope. So, he killed himself.

When we allow our minds to continue to be focused on our regrets or mistakes and we don't remember the love of Jesus, the love He has shown to us, it can lead us to do harmful things to ourselves. If you have been struggling with suicidal thoughts and not seeing there is a way out, I want you to remember there is always hope.

Jesus demonstrated how priceless you are to him by giving up everything for you. He loves you so intensely and wants you to remember this. So, when Satan is attacking your mind like he attacked Judas, reach out for help. Call the Suicide Hotline (988) or 800-273-8255 for help.

Remember you are loved, you are seen, and God loves you with everlasting love.

In all, we have to ask ourselves do we want to be like Peter who lost hope at one time but always held on to the fact that he was loved which led him to regain his hope. Or, Like Judas who took his relationship with Jesus for granted and didn't really understand fully how much he was loved, which led him to not return to the love when he betrayed Him. I truly pray we become more like Peter and remember we are loved more than what we can understand and allow this love to heal our hearts.

The Power of God's Cleansing

2 Corinthians 7:1 – *"Let us purify ourselves from everything that contaminates body and spirit, perfecting holiness out of reverence for God."*

Spiritual cleansing isn't about clearing an aura—it's about removing anything that separates us from God. Whether it's sinful habits, toxic thoughts, or negative influences, we must surrender them to Christ. He is our **living water**, washing away all impurities and filling us with new life (John 7:38).

Steps to Spiritual Renewal

Repent and Seek God's Forgiveness

"If we confess our sins, he is faithful and just to forgive us our sins and to cleanse us from all unrighteousness." – 1 John 1:9

"Therefore confess your sins to each other and pray for each other so that you may be healed. The prayer of a righteous person is powerful and effective." –James 5:16

Take time to confess anything that is weighing on your heart. God is always ready to forgive and restore you. Also, find a safe person you can confess your sins with and who is willing to pray for you and with you. As a disciple, having accountability partners is important and helpful so that we can walk with each other in the midst of these times.

Fill Your Mind with God's Word

"Do not conform to the pattern of this world, but be transformed by the renewing of your mind." – Romans 12:2

Read and meditate on Scripture daily to replace negative thoughts with God's truth. Also, speak them out loud so that you can hear the word of God. Remember Romans 10:17 says, *"So then faith comes by hearing, and hearing by the word of God."*

Pray for God's Strength

"Create in me a clean heart, O God, and renew a right spirit within me." – Psalm 51:10
Ask God to purify your heart and strengthen your spirit. He will equip you with peace and wisdom. Be vulnerable during your prayer time with the Lord. Sometimes we think that He already knows what we are going through, but He is a great Father and wants

to hear it from you. Cry out to Him and allow Him to comfort and help you.

Let God's Light Shine Through You

"Let your light shine before others, that they may see your good deeds and glorify your Father in heaven." – Matthew 5:16

"If we claim to have fellowship with him and yet walk in the darkness, we lie and do not live out the truth. But if we walk in the light, as he is in the light, we have fellowship with one another, and the blood of Jesus, his Son, purifies us from all sin." - 1 John 1:6-7

Remember when we are trying to hide things, we are not trying to be exposed to the light, which blocks us from growing closer to God and to others. When we allow ourselves to be vulnerable and open about the sins in our lives, our hearts are cleansed and our lives will reflect God's love and goodness to others.

A Prayer for Cleansing

"Heavenly Father, I come before You, asking for a clean heart and a renewed spirit. Wash away anything that separates me from You—my fears, doubts, and sins. Fill me with Your Holy Spirit and guide me in Your truth.

Gwendolyn Miller, MA, LPC-MHSP

Let my life reflect Your love and holiness. In Jesus' name, Amen."

Final Thought

Spiritual cleansing is not a ritual—it's a relationship with Christ. When we surrender our hearts to Him, He renews us completely. Instead of seeking worldly solutions, let us seek **the true and living God** who purifies, strengthens, and restores.

CHAPTER 6

Spiritual Thinkings

Synopsis

When you're able to have positive thoughts regardless what is going on – when you are able to see God in all individuals and in all situations – you are well on your way to spiritual health.

Notions

A lot of times we spend hours and hours dwelling and ruminating on the damaging and fearful things in our lives. Rather, our focus and attention needs to be on the favorable, the good, and on thoughts that will move us in the right direction. Read one of these statements to yourself each day -- and dwell on it.

If you pay attention to the dark, you'll never find the light.

A joyful person walks in the present, free from the burdens of the past and the worries of the future, trusting fully in the Lord's plan.

(**Matthew 6:34** – *"Therefore do not worry about tomorrow, for tomorrow will worry about itself. Each day has enough trouble of its own."*)

Too much thinking and dissecting just makes any issue worse. Today is a fantastic day – live it in the here and now.

Why do little youngsters think ghosts, goblins, and monsters are real? As grownups, we know they aren't. Your thoughts aren't "real" in either the sense that you —produce‖ and reinforce them -- and the emotions that go along with them. Your thoughts are only what you decide to trust in and continually reinforce in your brain.

For instance, you're sitting alone in the dark in your home. You're down, depressed and thinking damaging thoughts. All of a sudden the phone rings and it's an acquaintance you haven't talked to in 6 years. You become alert, your mood picks up, and you've a nice conversation. Then, after you've hung up, you get depressed again and fall back into a blue mood. How come?

Hint: Even though we don't feel it – we have more might over our thoughts than we believe. We may decide to stay "up" after the phone call by doing everything we can to keep from dropping off back into the quicksand of contemplation and despair.

If your thoughts start to change, you'll feel better.

If you act in spite of your feelings, your beliefs and emotions will follow behind.

2 Corinthians 10:5 – *"We demolish arguments and every pretension that sets itself up against the knowledge of God, and we take captive every thought to make it obedient to Christ."* (NIV)

The Bible says that we have the power to demolish strongholds and the power to take captive of every thought and make them obedient to Christ. Ya'll, can I tell you a secret? Satan doesn't want you to know the power you have in you when you have the Holy Spirit living in you. I truly pray we all grow more and more in understanding our power and the power of God that is in us and with us.

Your emotions and behavior are produced by your thoughts.

Unhappiness can't exist on its own. It happens because of thoughts, which may be altered.

Your past thoughts are about issues that are no longer true. That bad experience occurred yesterday (in the past) and is over. It's at peace and exists solely in your brain. Now is a fresh day, a better day, and fretting about the past simply dooms us in the here and now. It's how you process it now that makes a difference.

You are a thought-producing machine. When you recognize this, you are able to start to slow your thoughts down and let your anxieties and fears rest. Your automatic damaging thoughts are only thoughts; they're not real.

Our inclination is to think a bit too much and to paralyze ourselves with our contemplations. We have a choice: recognize what we're doing to ourselves, get up, find a distraction, and do something interesting (favorable).

Happy individuals understand that to enjoy life, you live it -- you don't think about it.

Watch a roomful of preschool youngsters. They're enjoying life as they're centered on the moment and are not thinking of it. They're immersed and engaged in living.

Analysis produces paralysis.

Anxiety killing you? Quit thinking about it, take that step, and simply do it.

Thoughts grow with attention. If you center on damaging thoughts, they'll grow and grow and get bigger. If you center on your progress and the fresh thoughts you're learning, they'll grow stronger and take "automatic" control.

Philippians 4:6 Do not be anxious about anything, but in every situation, by prayer and petition, with thanksgiving, present your requests to God. And the peace of God, which transcends all understanding, will guard your hearts and your minds in Christ Jesus.

This scripture can be used as a road map to help you break through anxiety. Paul is telling us not to be anxious and how we can overcome it. We overcome anxiety by prayer and petitions, with thanksgiving. Focusing on thanksgiving and submitting your worries to God helps you to rest in His hands and know He is in control. When we worry, we are struggling with wanting to be in control. But guess what, we have to learn what we can control and learn how to let go and trust God with what we can't control.

Even if you understand and know why you have a problem, this won't help you in solving it. Going over and over the reasons for your issue is like pouring salt in an open sore.

The only factor making you distressed is your own thoughts. Relax, eject them, and let them go.

Healing: Inside Out And Outside In

When you observe self-limiting and self-defeating thoughts playing again and again in your mind, state, "STOP! I will not give you any more power over me! I have greater things to accomplish!"

CHAPTER 7

Forgiving Other People

Synopsis

When you comprehend how the power of forgiveness may release you from negative states of affairs, it will become one of your most potent ongoing practices. This includes forgiving other people, situations, and likewise yourself.

Let Go

Forgiveness is a gift you give to yourself. It is not something you do for somebody else. It is not complicated. It's simple. Merely identify the situation to be forgiven and ask yourself: "Am I willing to squander my energy further on this issue?" If the answer is "No", then that's it! All is forgiven.

Forgiveness is an act of the imagination. It dares you to envisage a greater future, one that's based on the blessed possibility that your anguish won't be the final word on the issue. It challenges you to forfeit your destructive thoughts about the situation and to trust in the possibility of a greater future. It builds up confidence that you may survive the pain and develop from it.

Telling somebody is a bonus! It is not essential for forgiveness to start the process that heals the harm. Forgiveness has little or nothing to do with a different individual because forgiveness is an inner matter.

Choice is forever present in forgiveness. You don't have to forgive AND there are consequences. Refusing to forgive by holding on to the anger, bitterness and a sense of betrayal may make your own life deplorable. A vindictive mentality produces bitterness and lets the betrayer claim one more victim. There's nothing so bad that can't be forgiven. Nothing!

"The weak may never forgive. Forgiveness is the attribute of the strong." Mahatma Gandhi

The biggest misconception about forgiveness is the belief that forgiving the offense, like an affair, means that you excuse it. Not true. As a matter of fact, we may only forgive what we understand to be wrong. Forgiveness doesn't mean that you have to reconcile with somebody who poorly treated you.

Another misconception is that it depends upon whether the individual who did you wrong apologizes, wants you back, or alters his or her ways. If another person's miserable behavior were the primary determinant for your healing, then the cruel and selfish individuals in your life would retain power over you indefinitely. Forgiveness is the experience of discovering peace inside and may neither be compelled nor stopped by another. I trust that to withhold forgiveness is to decide to continue to remain the victim. Remember, you forever have a choice.

When you forgive, you do it for you, not for the other. The individual you've never forgiven. . . owns you! How about an affair? Simply because you choose to forgive, doesn't mean you have to stay in the relationship. That's only and always your choice. The choice to forgive is only and forever yours.

When you feel that forgiveness is essential, don't forgive for "their" sake. Do it for yourself! It would be great if they'd come to you and ask forgiveness but you have to accept the fact that some individuals will never do that. That's their choice. They don't have to be forgiven. They did what they did and that is it - except for the aftermaths, which THEY have to live with.

The hurts won't heal until you forgive! Recovery from wrongful conduct that produces genuine forgiveness takes time. For a few, it might take years. Don't rush it. Constantly reliving your hurt feelings gives the individual who caused you pain power over you. Rather than mentally replaying your hurt, it helps to center your energy on the healing, not the hurt!

Compassion is among the key ingredients of forgiveness. Learn to seek and appreciate the love, beauty and kindness around you. It's there, and you might have to alter your thinking and behavior to discover it. To have compassion for other people, you have to first have compassion for yourself.

Fit relationships are not possible without forgiveness! You can't have a loving and rewarding relationship with anybody else, much less yourself, if you continue to hold on to things that occurred in the past. Regardless of the situation, making peace with past love partners, your parents, youngsters, your boss or anybody who you think might have "done you wrong" is the only way to better your chances of a "healthy" relationship with yourself or anybody else for that matter! It isn't possible to truly be present and available to a fresh relationship till you heal the hurt and upsets of the past.

Gwendolyn Miller, MA, LPC-MHSP

Forgiving somebody else is to agree inside yourself to overlook the wrong they've committed against you and to move on with your life. It's the only way. It entails cutting them some slack. "What?" you say! "Cut them some slack after what THEY did to me? Never!" Let go! March on!

Non-forgiveness keeps you in the battle. Being willing to forgive may bring a sense of peace and well-being. It lifts anxiousness and delivers you from depression. It may enhance your self-regard and give you hope. Forgiveness is a journey. You might never forget AND you may decide to forgive. You may forgive and tomorrow you might feel the pain all over once again. As life goes on and you decide to remember and feel the pain, then is the time to over again remember that you've already forgiven. Mentally forgive again if necessary, then move onward. When we allow it, time may dull the vividness of the memory of the hurt; the memory will finally fade. Always remember that you're human. Occasionally individuals do and say hurtful things. It's crucial to center on what you've done to learn from the experience.

Forgiveness is a creative act that changes us from captives of the past to liberated individuals at peace with our memories. It isn't forgetfulness, but it demands accepting the promise that the future may be more than dwelling on memories of past harm. There's no future in the past. You may never live in

Healing: Inside Out And Outside In

the present and produce a new and exciting future for yourself if you always stay stuck in the past.

Start again! It's truly impossible to begin new and to make clear, healthy, life giving choices till we have let go of past injuries, confusion and resentments. Old injuries have a drawing power and pull our attention to them over and over, claiming energy and hope from us, preventing us from beginning again. Old wounds raise awful specters of the same thing occurring again in the future. For this reason, it is so crucial to spend time understanding the true nature of forgiveness, and what it truly entails.

To forgive means to "give up", to release. It likewise means to restore oneself to basic goodness and health. Once we forgive, we're willing to forfeit resentment, revenge and obsession. We're willing to reconstruct faith not only in ourselves, but in life itself. The inability or unwillingness to do this, causes damage in the one who's holding onto the anger.

If you're at war with other people, you can't be at peace with yourself. You may let go. . . and forgive! It takes no strength to release. . . only bravery. Life either expands or contracts in direct proportion to your bravery to forgive. Your decision to forgive or not to forgive either moves you closer to what you want or further away from it. There's no middle ground. Change is constant.

Gwendolyn Miller, MA, LPC-MHSP

Want peacefulness? Forgive. The same power you utilize to hold on (to not forgive), is the same power you need to produce a fresh and exciting life. Forgiveness is the most crucial single process that brings peace to our soul and harmony to our life. All of us, at some point in our lives, have been injured and wounded by the actions or words of another. Occasionally the grievances have been so capital we thought, "no way, this I can't forgive!" Resentment and hostility may run so deep that forgiveness becomes really hard. We believe we have a right to our outrage!

But, living from resentment takes such effort. It produces an enormous void in and around us. All the toxic feelings of hate and bitterness remain suppressed inside and eventually seep into all the areas of our life with the result that we get bitter, angry, distressed and frustrated. And so, living from forgiveness becomes an essential.

Not that this is simple; it isn't. But we can't keep ourselves in the flow of good if we hold some other in un-forgiveness. Forgiveness isn't something we have to do, but something we must leave flow through us. When we step away from the awareness of our human nature, and allow the divine or the higher powers grace to express through us, to forgive through us, we may at that point, feel the beaming and warm rays of the flow of divine love breaking up all hurt, all resentment, all sense of injustice. We get aware that we're free and we may project that love outward into our world.

Forgiveness helps you move ahead. No one benefits from forgiveness more than the one who forgives! Afford yourself the gift of forgiveness. The very word forgiveness is built upon the root word give. Forgiveness frees people from your criticism and likewise frees you from being imprisoned by your own damaging judgments. It isn't surrender, but a witting decision to cease to harbor bitterness. In affect, it takes the poison out of your body. It cleans your system of the poison that will certainly fester and induce illness and continued misery if not released. You can't take the poison and expect somebody else to die. They'll go on with their life and you'll be the only one to continue to suffer.

Forgiveness is the key to your own happiness. Forgiving somebody else takes moral bravery. Its power may change misery into happiness in a moment. Forgiveness means deciding to release, move on, and favor the positive. Forgiveness is a sort of love inside the context of a personal crisis. To forgive is, in a way, to love one's enemy. When forgiveness is afforded because you think you ought to, it no longer is forgiveness but an act of self-concern.

The act of forgiveness constitutes a mental bath, releasing something that may only poison us inside.

It produces the freedom to create a fresh future beginning today!

Before I close this chapter on forgiveness, I want to look at a story in the Bible that shares how Jesus sees forgiveness. Let's look at Matthew 18:21-35 (NIV).

"**21** Then Peter came up and said to Him, "Lord, how many times shall my brother sin against me and I *still* forgive him? Up to seven times?" **22** Jesus *said to him, "I do not say to you, up to seven times, but up to [w]seventy-seven times.

23 "For this reason the kingdom of heaven [x]is like a king who wanted to settle accounts with his slaves. **24** And when he had begun to settle *them*, one who owed him [y]ten thousand talents was brought to him. **25** But since he [z]did not have *the means* to repay, his master commanded that he be sold, along with his wife and children and all that he had, and repayment be made. **26** So the slave fell *to the ground* and prostrated himself before him, saying, 'Have patience with me and I will repay you everything.' **27** And the master of that slave felt compassion, and he released him and forgave him the [aa]debt. **28** But that slave went out and found one of his fellow slaves who owed him a hundred [ab] denarii; and he seized him and *began* to choke *him*, saying, 'Pay back what you owe!' **29** So his fellow slave fell *to the ground* and *began* to plead with him, saying, 'Have patience with me and I will repay you.' **30** But

Healing: Inside Out And Outside In

he was unwilling, [ac]and went and threw him in prison until he would pay back what was owed. ³¹ So when his fellow slaves saw what had happened, they were deeply grieved and came and reported to their master all that had happened. ³² Then summoning him, his master *said to him, 'You wicked slave, I forgave you all that debt because you pleaded with me. ³³ Should you not also have had mercy on your fellow slave, in the same way that I had mercy on you?' ³⁴ And his master, moved with anger, handed him over to the [ad]torturers until he would repay all that was owed him. ³⁵ My heavenly Father will also do the same to you, if each of you does not forgive his brother from your [ae]heart."

In this story, the unmerciful servant wasn't able to pay back what he owed, but the king forgave him all of his debt. Can you imagine this? Not having the money to pay the debt back and being forgiven of it? What did the man do?

Instead of being merciful himself, showing someone else kindness because he was shown kindness, or withholding punishment even though he deserved it, he refused to forgive the debt of someone else who owed him. Think about this ya'll. God is the King. We have done so much against Him. You can look at your own life and see how much you deserve the punishment you were owed. I deserve the punishment I was owed, but God in His great mercy, forgave you and me. He didn't hold our wages against

Gwendolyn Miller, MA, LPC-MHSP

us but cleared our slate as if we no longer owed Him anything. In fact, He paid the cost for us by giving up His son to die, taking on the punishment that was due to us. Wrap your minds around this. So, what are we saying when we are so unyielding in holding grudges and not forgiving others? What is the message we are saying to Jesus, to our Father?

In order to truly forgive, we have to remember what we have done to our Father and what Jesus did for us to be forgiven by Him. Remember the cross. Remember the torture Jesus went through for you. Remember and ask yourself, is holding on to this grudge more than that? Whatever someone has done to you, it doesn't compare to what we did to Jesus. Yes, we put Jesus on the cross. He didn't have to go, but he chose to go so that we could experience mercy and forgiveness. This is why God takes unforgiveness so personally and why we will not be forgiven if we don't forgive. Who are we not to forgive and hold someone else captive when the Father who created all things decided to set us free and forgive us.

In summary, forgiveness frees your heart. I remember watching Once Upon A Time, and there was a scene where Snow White's son took out his heart to give to Peter Pan, who was evil. Snow White's son's heart was so pure and loving, but when we have unforgiveness in our hearts or bitterness, it's like taking our hearts and allowing evil to have it, to harden it.

Healing: Inside Out And Outside In

What happens when our hearts are hardened with bitterness, it sickens us and can lead to health problems and toxic relationships.

Forgiveness cleanses your heart, clears the slate so that you can be released from the burden of unforgiveness, free to enjoy this life God has given you. Remember, unforgiveness is like you drinking poison expecting the other person to die. Let's stop drinking the poison and free ourselves so we can truly live this life to the fullest, walking in the light and love of Jesus.

CHAPTER 8

Attitude of Appreciation

Synopsis

This is an enormously powerful spiritual wellness drill. Say prayers of thanksgiving on a steady basis. When you're grateful for the good that you already have it paves the way for more good to flow into your life.

What do you have to be glad about? Getting to this gratitude, all the same, isn't always so simple. Being able to authentically express appreciation requires you to shift your focus away from the things that are damaging and toward those things that you feel grateful for.

And as you already know, it's really simple to forget to be thankful for all the astonishing things we experience on a daily basis.

Appreciation

Many of us living in western society tend to center on what we don't have. We believe we don't have adequate money, we don't have adequate time, we don't have the mate we're seeking etc. And in this exercise -- which may frankly dominate our daily thinking if we're not careful -- we tend to disregard those astonishing things we do have. So the more we may step back and have a look at what we already experience that's valuable to us, the more we may center on gratitude and the more we may accelerate our own inside healing as a result.

Here's a list of a few of the things for which you might find plenty of appreciation:

- Your relationship with God and with Jesus.
- Your loved ones.
- Your freedoms (freedom of speech, and so forth.)
- Your intelligence, awareness and consciousness.
- Your memories! (Life without memories would be freaky...)
- Sunshine and nature -- the great outdoors.

- Food and seeds, a few of the many remarkable presents from Mother Nature.
- Your occupation, business or job which supplies the revenue you require.
- Your curiousness and want to learn new things.
- Your wellness. Even if it isn't perfect, you might be grateful for the health you have.
- Your pets / creature companions.

In fact, if you consider it, there are likely a great many things for which you may feel great gratitude -- the little plants in your windowsill, the knowledge about wellness that you've accumulated through studying, and even the fact that the sun will indeed arise tomorrow.

Take a couple of minutes and consider what you're grateful for. You might even wish to take a couple of moments to jot some notes for yourself. With your list of those matters you're grateful for, I'd like to invite you to allow just one minute per day (or more, if you wish) to recap that list, to verbalize your gratitude and to very take in your gratefulness for those things that you do have.

Literally say it aloud: "I'm grateful for the garden in my back yard and the chance to grow a little portion of my own food" for instance. In just sixty seconds per day, if used daily, you'll produce an attitude of appreciation, which will lighten your mood and uplift your daily experience of life as it lets you refocus your attention on those matters you appreciate instead of those things you may despise.

Each type of energy that you express to somebody else is reflected in your own interior experience. So if you express hate toward another individual or subject, there's an element of that energy that's likewise expressed internally in that instant. To detest somebody else is to subject yourself to some reflection of that own hatred, put differently.

At the same time, to love something else -- or to express gratefulness toward it -- causes a reflection of that favorable energy to be felt inside yourself, too.

Lastly, let's talk about anger. Anger is a destructive emotion as it induces stress, adrenal depletion and tension throughout the body. But you may learn to replace anger (or other damaging emotions) with appreciation, and anger can't coexist with appreciation. In that way, appreciation may begin to nudge out the other damaging emotions you may be experiencing. This doesn't mean you have to run around blindly grateful for everything without discerning times when critique or anger may be called for, but the more you may find the appreciation in daily things, the more you'll set off and support your body's inner healing procedures.

WRAPPING UP

Living a life as a disciple of Jesus and with biblical spiritual wellness calls for bravery, discipline, and love for God. When we strive to live our lives for God and allow Him to be the center of our lives, He will help us overcome and work through our struggles. Remember, as Paul said in *2 Corinthians 5:14 For Christ's love compels us, because we are convinced that one died for all, and therefore all died.*

ABOUT THE AUTHOR

Gwendolyn (Melika) Miller is a licensed professional counselor and pastoral counselor in Tennessee. Gwendolyn is certified in Dialectical Behavior Therapy and Mindfulness practice. Her practice is called Love Abundantly Counseling, Inc. and she works with women and men who are struggling with depression, anxiety, trauma, and other life issues. She merges the Bible with evidence-based practices and helps her clients walk through their healing process. Gwendolyn also has a ministry called Love Abundantly Ministry and she uses her 27 years of experience as a single living as a disciple of Jesus to help other women overcome obstacles that are blocking them from growing deeper in intimacy with God. Through Love Abundantly Ministry, Gwendolyn has led webinars and retreats over the years and has impacted many lives. Gwendolyn has also spoken at single conferences and retreats around the country.

Gwendolyn Miller, MA, LPC-MHSP

Additionally, Gwendolyn is the author of a book called "40 years a Virgin: Why the wait-Promoting Purity in a World of Promiscuity" which is under her name Melika Miller and is found on Amazon.

Lastly, Gwendolyn is a musician and a Soul Music artist under the name Meliks Miller where her music is available on Spotify, Youtube, and other digital sites.

Follow her on IG:

@LoveAbundantlyMinistry
@LoveAbundantlyCounseling
@MelikaMiller

Website: www.loveabundantlyministry.com
and www.melikamiller.net

www.ingramcontent.com/pod-product-compliance
Lightning Source LLC
Chambersburg PA
CBHW020548080526
44583CB00013B/1049